I-SPY

DINOSAURS

& PREHISTORIC ANIMALS

This book belongs to:

I began this book on: (DATE)

D1396059

I made my first I-Spy on: (DATE)

I sent off for my badge on: (DATE)

To get you started on the 1000 points you need for a badge, here are a few easy spots you can make now.

In the 'Theropods of the Jurassic' what feature of the skull is shared by crocodiles, pterosaurs, and dinosaurs?
5 points for a right answer

'Ornithopods of the Cretaceous': Waterhouse Hawkins's model of Iguanodon is incorrect in two main features. What are they?
5 points for a right answer

Among the 'Early Armoured and Horned Dinosaurs' how many toes make up the hoof-like foot of Monoclonius?
5 points for a right answer

Why is one of the 'Horned Dinosaurs' called Triceratops?
5 points for a right answer

Answers on page 48

Dinosaurs are perhaps the best known of all fossil reptiles. They are often thought of as huge and fierce but all shapes and sizes are known, and their eating habits were quite varied. Remains of dinosaurs are known from all the continents except Antarctica. They first appeared some 225 million years ago and died out 65 million years ago at the end of a period in Earth's history called the Cretaceous. The earliest dinosaurs have been found from the southern lands of South Africa and South America but they seem to have spread northwards quite soon into North America, Europe, and Asia. Dinosaur bones are usually found in sediments that were deposited in lakes or along the banks of rivers. They are not common in rocks formed from sediments laid down in the sea. Skeletons with their joints intact are surprisingly common in some localities known as *lägerstatten*. The picture here is of a sauropod find in central West Africa.

*I-Spy **35** for a field example*

In the state of Utah in the United States, a wonderful discovery was made of enormous bones. They proved to be the bones of Jurassic dinosaurs and are among the best-known examples in the world. Skilled scientists are still cleaning and preserving the dinosaur bones that were exposed on a quarry face. Now there is a large visitor centre in the region that once yielded skeletons of *Apatosaurus* 23 metres (76 ft) long.

*I-Spy **50** for a visit to Vernal, Utah*

When Richard Owen first wrote about dinosaurs in the early part of the nineteenth century, his ideas of their size and shape were rather different from what scientists believe today. Owen commissioned Waterhouse Hawkins to build models of *Megalosaurus*, *Iguanodon*, and *Hylaeosaurus*. Generally, the sizes of the models were approximately correct but we now know that *Megalosaurus* and *Iguanodon* walked on their hind limbs and that *Hylaeosaurus* (shown here) was a four-footed armoured dinosaur.

*I-Spy **15** for Hylaeosaurus*

Over the last 150 years, we have learned a great deal about dinosaurs. In fact, museums now exhibit models that can move. They are so life-like and noisy that they seem to take us on a journey into prehistory. The outer 'skin' covers a cleverly engineered frame driven by electric motors.

*I-Spy **10** for a moving model*

Ornithosuchus

The ancestors of dinosaurs are called 'tooth-in-socket' reptiles, or thecodontians. *Ornithosuchus* was one of the earliest dinosaurs, an early relative of *Coelurosaurus* and *Tyrannosaurus*. It was a meat-eater that ran on its hind legs. Just 3 metres (almost 10 ft) long and 1 metre (just over 3 ft) tall, it had very sharp teeth and could run quickly. *Ornithosuchus* has been found in the Triassic rocks of Scotland. Plant-eating dinosaurs also appeared during the Triassic, with *Fabrosaurus* and *Heterodontosaurus* known from finds in the southern hemisphere. *Ornithosuchus* is rare, and you will have to study museum collections and displays carefully to I-Spy it.

I-Spy for **35**

Saltopus

This tiny dinosaur has also been found in Upper Triassic rocks of Scotland so it lived about 210 million years ago. It measured only 60 centimetres (2 ft) long and was a biped, that is, it ran on its hind legs. Like *Ornithosuchus*, it could run quickly. Its short, strong arms and strong-fingered hands helped it to grip the prey animals it caught after a short chase. *Saltopus* may have eaten early mammals, such as *Morganucodon*, which look rather mouse-like. *Saltopus* is another rare dinosaur because its delicate skeleton was so easily destroyed after its death.

*I-Spy for **35***

Footprints in the Rocks

Dinosaur footprints are often found in the red sandstones and mudstones of the Triassic Period. The red colour of these rocks indicates that the environment was dry and desert-like. Small and very large prints have been found suggesting that there was a variety of dinosaurs living at the time. Not all of these dinosaurs have have been preserved as body fossils.

*I-Spy for **15***

GIANT DINOSAURS

The giants of the dinosaur world were the sauropods. These were plant-eating monsters that grew to lengths of as much as 30 metres (100 ft). The heaviest were *Brachiosaurus* and *Supersaurus* weighing in at over 80 tonnes; *Supersaurus* was probably at least 15 metres (almost 50 ft) tall, too!

The sauropods can be divided into two groups, the brachiosaurs and the apatosaurs. Brachiosaurs have long front legs and are tall at the shoulder whereas apatosaurs have long back legs and tend to lean forward.

The Jurassic (208-144 million years ago) landscape was forested with firs,

conifers, cycads (palm-like plants), and the similar bennettitaleans. Ferns and horsetails covered the ground and bordered lakes and river banks. The sauropods fed on the soft plants of the lakes or on the delicate leaves on the high branches of the trees that surrounded more open countryside. They shared their habitat with *Stegosaurus* and its relative *Kentrosaurus*. These plated dinosaurs were also plant-eaters. *Stegosaurus* may have been able to control its body temperature using the plates that run along its back.

I-Spy 25 for Brachiosaurus

I-Spy 15 for Stegosaurus

I-Spy 25 for Apatosaurus

Stegosaurus

Skeletons of *Stegosaurus* are well known from the Late Jurassic of the western United States of America. *Stegosaurus* was 6-7 metres (20-23 ft) long and weighed 2 tonnes. The plates on its back were arranged in two, slightly offset rows. *I-Spy 25 for a stegosaur skeleton*

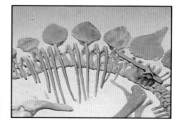

Diplodocus Skeleton

Diplodocus, the 'double-beam' lizard, is one of the sauropods that had short front legs. It lived during Late Jurassic to Early Cretaceous times some 150-100 million years ago. Full-grown animals reached lengths of 26 metres (85 ft) and weighed between 10 and 12 tonnes. *Diplodocus* had a long neck and very long tail. Its teeth were located at the front of its jaws, and it is likely that the animal fed on soft plant material in lakes or big ponds. Surprisingly, the skull measured only 65 centimetres (26 inches) long. The body was deep, like that of an elephant, but *Diplodocus* had no tusks to defend itself; this task was left to the whiplash of the tail.

I-Spy for **15**

Model *Diplodocus*

You can quite often find reconstructions of *Diplodocus* in theme parks or in museums. In the Dinosaur Garden at Vernal, Utah in the United States, this model, built by Elbert H Porter, is based on skeletons found locally in Jurassic sedimentary rocks. Close relatives of the American *Diplodocus* have been found recently on the Isle of Wight off the south coast of England.

I-Spy for **20**
Double for a Vernal model

Animatronics

The motorized models of *Diplodocus* that you can now find in several museums are similar to the Vernal reconstruction. The 'skin' is flexible, however; the neck moves, and the mouth opens to utter a deep sound. The sauropods are thought to have lived in family groups, the young cared for by the mother.

I-Spy for 15

Ornitholestes

Ornitholestes was a comparatively small dinosaur with a 'lizard-like' hip. It was a theropod, a meat-eater closely related to the Triassic *Coelurosaurus*. It was about 2 metres (6½ ft) long and weighed between 18 and 32 kilograms (40-70 lb). The front limbs were short but strong, and probably helped the animal to catch and hold its prey. *Ornitholestes* ran on its hind legs and used the long tail to help it balance. It is likely that this dinosaur fed on insects or small reptiles and mammals. It may have been a scavenger, too, eating any scraps left behind by *Megalosaurus* or other large meat-eaters.

I-Spy for **35**

Allosaurus

Whereas *Ornitholestes* was small and agile, *Allosaurus* was huge and powerful. Big males reached more than 9 metres (30 ft) in length and weighed several tonnes. Although it was smaller than *Tyrannosaurus*, *Allosaurus* was possibly the most effective of the meat-eating, lizard-hipped dinosaurs. One blow from its powerful leg would stun most animals, and its massive jaws would make any struggle to survive useless. When moving at speed, *Allosaurus* could cover 6 metres (20 ft) with every stride.
I-Spy for 35

Allosaurus Skull

The skull of *Allosaurus* was armed with many sharp, dagger-like teeth. The jaws opened to a huge gape, and one bite would rip an enormous chunk of flesh. The presence of two openings in the skull behind the eye is a common feature shared by crocodiles, pterosaurs (prehistoric flying reptiles), and dinosaurs.
I-Spy for 25

Megalosaurus Bones and Skeleton

The word *Megalosaurus* simply means 'big lizard'. Large males were 4 to 5 metres (13-16 ft) tall and about 12 metres (almost 40 ft) long. They weighed between 2 and 4 tonnes, and hunted on the borders of forests and around the edges of lakes. Not only has *Megalosaurus* been known longer than any other dinosaur, it was probably one of the most successful, and lived through the Jurassic and early Cretaceous. Look for its bones in the museums of Europe.

I-Spy for **15**

Megalosaurus at Crystal Palace

Of the three dinosaurs first exhibited in the grounds of the Crystal Palace at Sydenham, south London, *Megalosaurus* is the most colourful in two different senses. This is not only because the model is painted but also because of its early history. The first bone of *Megalosaurus* to be discovered was thought at the time to be part of a human thigh bone. The

fossil was first illustrated in 1676, and *Megalosaurus* also has the distinction of being the first of the three giant reptiles – later to be called dinosaurs – to be described scientifically.

I-Spy for **15**

Coelurus

Throughout Upper Jurassic times, tiny scavengers and meat-eaters, such as *Coelurus*, were common across the lands of western North America. They fed on insects, small reptiles, the early mammals, and occasionally leapt to catch a small pterosaur that was also in search of food.
I-Spy for 25

Segisaurus

Wherever giants, such as *Allosaurus* and *Megalosaurus* fed, there were rich pickings for tiny scavengers like *Segisaurus*. Nimble and alert, these little dinosaurs would skirt the carcass until the chance came to dart in, rip and snatch a piece of meat, and then feed quietly somewhere else. *Segisaurus* is closely related to the coelurosaurs, and it held its food using the three strong fingers on each hand. Always on the look-out, it could easily catch a small mammal or lizard that left the safety of the undergrowth.
I-Spy for 50

Compsognathus Skeleton

The name of this dinosaur means 'strutting jaw'. With a head only about 8 centimetres (3 inches) long and a total body length of just 65 centimetres (26 inches), it was about the size of a large chicken. Surprisingly, perhaps, its skeleton was similar to that of the first bird *Archaeopteryx*, and most scientists now believe that small dinosaurs, such as *Compsognathus*, were the true ancestors of the birds. *Compsognathus* lived during the Late Jurassic about 150 million years ago. It fed on insects and small reptiles and amphibians. The area where it lived would have bordered a shallow sea, and its remains are beautifully preserved in the very fine sediments laid down on the sea floor.

I-Spy for 25

Archaeopteryx Model

Sometimes referred to as 'Archie', *Archaeopteryx* is the earliest known bird. Because of the limited number of skeletons that have been discovered so far, they are probably the most valuable fossils in the world. Like *Compsognathus*, it had a delicate skeleton, but it had the beginnings of a wishbone, and well-developed feathers covered the wings and tail. It is likely that *Archaeopteryx* could fly short distances, either launching itself from a branch or gliding short distances like a chicken. 'Ancient wing', as its name means, probably fed on insects, and large dragonflies, fossils of which have been preserved in the rocks of Solnhofen in southern German, and which would have made good eating.

I-Spy for 25

Archaeopteryx Skeleton

The delicate skeleton of *Archaeopteryx* is preserved in the Lithographic Limestone of the Jurassic of southern Germany. The stone was originally used in the printing industry. Nowadays, it is exploited more as a decorative stone. Shops and museums, however, sell the outstanding fossils preserved across the bedding surfaces.

I-Spy 50 for a skeleton,
15 for a cast

Struthiomimus

Struthiomimus was an ostrich dinosaur that lived during the Cretaceous in North America and Asia. It had beak-like, toothless jaws and a small head. The body was 4 metres (13 ft) long with a long neck and an even longer tail. *Struthiomimus* ran on its hind legs, and the shorter arms were used to hold food to the mouth. Ostrich dinosaurs were fast runners. The name *Struthiomimus* means 'ostrich imitator'. They fed on insects and small animals. They are also known to have been nest robbers, stealing eggs and young from unprotected dinosaur nests.

I-Spy for 35

Deinonychus

Few discoveries in recent times have created such interest as that of *Deinonychus* in 1964.

Deinonychus ('terrible-claw') grew to 3 metres (10 ft) in length and was more heavily built than the coelurosaurs. It had a large head, short neck and body, but a long, almost rigid tail. This combination gave *Deinonychus* excellent balance when it ran, and allowed it to deliver a fearful killing blow with the sickle-shaped claw developed on the second toe of each foot. The claw was 13 centimetres (5 inches) long. Look out for the claw and the bundles of bony rods that set the tail straight.

I-Spy for **25**

Tyrannosaurus rex

Of all the dinosaurs, *Tyrannosaurus rex*, 'king of the terrible lizards', is the best known. Models and casts of its skeleton can be found in most museums, and stories of its size and savage nature abound in children's books. *Tyrannosaurus rex* was probably the largest meat-eater ever to walk on land. It reached 12 metres (39 ft) in length, stood 5.6 metres (18 ft 4 in) tall, and weighed as much as 7 tonnes. It was quick but not very agile. One strike of its huge foot, however, would render its prey utterly helpless.

I-Spy for 5

Tyrannosaurus Skull

The skull of *T. rex* was 1.25 metres (4 ft) long. It was strongly built, and large muscles and sinews would have given the jaws massive biting power. The teeth were saw edged and 15 cm (6 in) in length. *T. rex* probably tore at the carcass of its victim using the huge clawed feet to push against.

I-Spy for 15

Trachodon

During the Late Cretaceous, the duck-billed dinosaurs, such as *Trachodon*, were very common across the western United States and Canada. They lived in family groups and herds, and were an important source of food for a hungry *Tyrannosaurus*. *Trachodon* was no midget, however, and large males weighed 3 or 4 tonnes. But they were peaceful plant-eaters, and used their batteries of flattened cheek teeth to crush and grind plants and seeds. The herding instinct would protect the majority but *Tyrannosaurus* would have been able to isolate young, old, or sick individuals. A lake might provide a safe haven but *T. rex* was often faster and much stronger than *Trachodon*.

I-Spy for 25

Hypsilophodon

The Early Cretaceous rocks of the Isle of Wight have yielded over twenty specimens of the 'high-ridge tooth' dinosaur *Hypsilophodon*. This bird-hipped dinosaur walked on its back legs and some scientists think it may have moved in a way similar to that of a kangaroo. *Hypsilophodon* was only 1.5 metres (5 ft) long and, like other ornithopod (bird-foot) dinosaurs, it was a plant-eater.
I-Spy for **25**

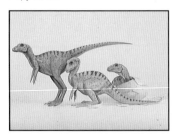

Dinosaur Eggs

There is evidence from many parts of the world that dinosaurs laid eggs and protected their young. Perhaps the most famous examples were discovered in the Flaming Cliffs area of the Gobi Desert and from the United States. It is likely that *Hypsilophodon* also laid eggs in clusters, and that the young hatched like young chicks.
I-Spy for **15**

Iguanodon

Apart from *Tyrannosaurus* and *Stegosaurus*, *Iguanodon* is perhaps one of the best known of all dinosaurs. Its fossils have been found in Europe, North Africa, and North America. The discovery, in 1877 and 1878, of the remains of thirty-one males, females, and juveniles near the Belgian town of Bernissart leads us to believe that *Iguanodon* was a herding animal. Numerous bones and trackways are also known from the Isle of Wight in southern England.

I-Spy for 5

Iguanodon at Crystal Palace

When Waterhouse Hawkins built the model of *Iguanodon* in the grounds of the Crystal Palace in south London, he was guided by Sir Richard Owen in determining the shape of the reconstruction. Owen thought that *Iguanodon* walked on all four legs and that the 'thumb nail' he had discovered was, in fact, a horn for the snout. About a dozen guests ate dinner inside the unfinished model of *Iguanodon* on New Year's Eve, 1853.

I-Spy for 15

Corythosaurus

Known as the 'helmet lizard', *Corythosaurus* had a hollow crest over the top of its head. We believe that the crest varied in size among males and females and that the dominant male had the largest. *Corythosaurus* grew to 9 metres (almost 30 ft) long and weighed about 4 tonnes. Like other duck-billed dinosaurs, the snout was broad and flattened. The teeth were leaf-like and overlapping to form a broad crushing surface. The tail of *Corythosaurus* was flattened at the sides and was probably used when the animal swam. Swimming was also aided by the webbed fingers on each hand. In contrast, the feet were rather hoof-like.

I-Spy for **25**

Hadrosaur Skeleton

The duck-billed dinosaurs, or hadrosaurs, were descended from *Iguanodon*. They were 'bird-footed' plant-eaters, and were deep chested with short arms. The tail had a particularly strong development of bony extensions, or spines, above and below the middle of each bony segment. These would provide ideal anchorage for the tendons and muscles needed to power the animal through the water when it swam.
*I-Spy for **15***

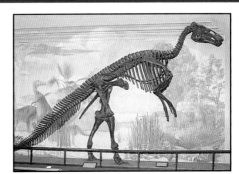

Parasaurolophus

How models have changed since the time of Waterhouse Hawkins! This reconstruction of a young specimen of *Parasaurolophus walkeri* is so detailed that it is life-like. The head of an adult *Parasaurolophus* was 3 metres (almost 10 ft) long. In the juvenile shown, the crest is only just beginning to grow.
*I-Spy for **25***

Scelidosaurus

Scelidosaurus, the 'limb lizard', is known from the Lower Jurassic rocks of southern England. It was four footed, heavily built, and up to 4 metres (13 ft) in length. The head was small and the body rather squat; it could be argued that *Scelidosaurus* was an early ankylosaur, or armoured dinosaur. First discovered in 1861, it is one of the earliest dinosaurs to be described by Sir Richard Owen. It was a peaceful plant-eater, its only protection the thick skin that carried several rows of plates. The jaw was weak and its teeth were designed for grinding food. It had little or no defence against predators like *Megalosaurus*.

I-Spy for **25**

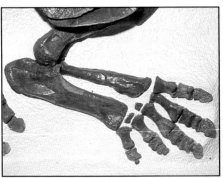

Monoclonius Limb

The limbs of the horned dinosaurs were short and strong. The front foot bore five toes which tended to form a hoof. This foot belonged to *Monoclonius nasicornis* the 'single-shoot' ceratopian. All of the horned dinosaurs were probably descended from the parrot-beaked *Psittacosaurus*.

I-Spy for **35**

Protoceratops

Protoceratops lived during the Upper Cretaceous in the area now known as Mongolia. Hundreds of skeletons have been recorded and many nests with eggs have been discovered in the same area. *Protoceratops* means 'first horned face'; it was 2 metres (6 ft 6 in) long and weighed about 180 kilograms (400 lb). The body was squat, and *Protoceratops* walked on all fours. The skull was very large, however, and there was a curved, bony frill or shield covering the neck. A parrot-like beak was typical of the horned dinosaurs and, in *Protoceratops*, the beak was narrow and sharp.

I-Spy 15 for Protoceratops *and 5 for eggs*

Triceratops

During the Upper Cretaceous, horned dinosaurs spread throughout Asia and the western area of North America. Their success is reflected in the great variety of different animals and through the huge numbers that roamed the open plains. We know that *Protoceratops* was the first of these animals but, about 70-80 million years ago, new types, such as *Monoclonius*, *Styracosaurus*, and *Triceratops*, were among the Upper Cretaceous dinosaur communities. *Triceratops*, with one horn on its snout and one above each brow, is perhaps the best known and the three horns are characteristic of this plant-eating giant.

Triceratops reached 7 metres (almost 23 feet) in length and weighed 8-9 tonnes. It looked like a rhinoceros but the huge, solid frill or shield gave it greater protection. Of course, it needed it – its deadly enemy was *Tyrannosaurus rex*! I-Spy **15** for a skeleton, **25** for a model

Monoclonius Skull and Frill

We have included the limb of *Monoclonius* or 'single shoot' on the previous double-page spread. It is worth noting, however, that its shield was quite short with a large hole on either side. The frill also had a rather rough, knobbly texture.
I-Spy for 35

Styracosaurus

Styracosaurus was one of the most spectacular of all the horned dinosaurs. Known as the 'spike lizard', its frill was decorated with six long spikes that extended backwards over the neck. At about 6 metres (almost 20 ft) long and weighing 6 or 7 tonnes, *Styracosaurus* was only slightly smaller than *Triceratops*.
I-Spy for 25

Ankylosaurus (opposite)

Ankylosaurus had a flexible armour and, like *Scolosaurus* (below), was a 'reptilian tank' from the Upper Cretaceous. Smaller than *Scolosaurus*, *Ankylosaurus* measured just 4.5 metres (almost 15 ft) in length. It was a very wide animal, however, and large males could measure 1.5 metres (5 ft) across the shoulders. Its armour lacked the spikes and nodes of that of its cousin but it completely covered the head, neck, back, and tail. The individual plates were oval or rounded in shape. The tail ended in a large bony swelling which provided the animal with its only defence apart from its armour. *Ankylosaurus* means 'stiff lizard' and the species *Ankylosaurus magiventris* is simply the 'stiff lizard with the huge belly'!

I-Spy for **25**

Scolosaurus

Scolosaurus was a low-slung, slow-moving heavyweight. It weighed several tonnes and waddled across the ground in a lizard-like manner. Large adults were 6 metres (almost 20 ft) long and the body was covered with flexible armour. There were spikes and nodes on each armoured segment, with the tallest spikes behind the head, over the hips, and at the end of the tail. The head was broad and the mouth rather beak-like with weak, blunt teeth. All the armoured dinosaurs were plant-eaters. They defended themselves against attack by sinking to the ground, the full armour deflecting the blows of an enraged *Tyrannosaurus*. In combat, the tail would have been used as a club, the strong spikes causing considerable injury to an unprotected foe.

I-Spy for **25**

w.francis phillips

BONE-HEADED LIZARDS

Pachycephalosaurus

The bone of the human skull is just several millimetres thick. By contrast, the bony thickening above the brain of *Pachycephalosaurus* was as much as 22.5 centimetres (9 inches) thick! It was also rough and knobbly, and many scientists believe it was used in defence or in the protection of its territory. Male mountain sheep and goats charge and butt one another during the mating season, and it is likely that pachycephalosaurs did the same. Imagine, however, two animals with skulls 60 centimetres (2 ft) long fighting during Late Cretaceous times; the noise would have been incredible.

Pachycephalosaurus grew to 4.6 metres (15 ft) long. Bone-headed dinosaurs have been discovered in western North America and China and Mongolia in Asia.

The mechanical models of *Pachycephalosaurus* that you can now find in museums and theme parks are quite spectacular. They are life-size and life-like – thank goodness they were plant-eaters! Like all dinosaurs, *Pachycephalosaurus* died out 65 million years ago.

*I-Spy for **35**, and **25** for a model*

In the Devonian, the variety and numbers of fishes reflected their ever-more important role in the seas and rivers. Many of the fishes shown here can be found in museums near outcrops of the Old Red Sandstone (Devonian). There are excellent collections in Glasgow and South Wales.

1 Pteraspis

Jawless fishes were the most primitive kinds of fishes. Among the best known is *Pteraspis*, a small fish [15 centimetres (6 in)] with a long, pointed snout and a well-developed head shield that continued over the body as a spine. Behind the shield, there were several small spines on the back. *Pteraspis* had no paired fins.
I-Spy for 5

2 Drepanaspis

This fish also lacked paired fins. Exceeding 30 centimetres (12 inches) in length, it was larger than *Pteraspis*. It had a similar tail, however, but the head shield was broad and shovel-like. *Drepanaspis* scavenged on the bottom.
I-Spy for 5

3 Psammolepis

Another jawless fish, *Psammolepis* also resembled *Pteraspis* but the head shield was slightly broader and had two ridges near the mid-line.
I-Spy for 5

4 Osteolepis

Osteolepis was a jawed fish. It had paired fins on the streamlined body which was covered in thick scales. The jaws were armed with many small teeth. They were active flesh-eaters and may have measured 25 centimetres (10 inches) long.
I-Spy for 15

5 Bothriolepis

Armoured fishes were abundant. *Bothriolepis* grew to about 30 centimetres (12 in) long. It had eyes on the top of its head, a rather flattened body, and a long tail. Oddly, the pectoral fins were contained in a crab-like casing.
I-Spy for 5

The first amphibian, *Ichthyostega*, appeared during the Late Devonian some 350 million years ago. In the Carboniferous, the coal swamplands provided ideal conditions for the expansion of the group. This scene, painted by the famous Czech artist Burian, illustrates a number of small amphibians: *Microbrachis* is lizard-like; *Branchiosaurus* is more like a salamander; and *Dolichosoma* has lost its limbs so that it is more snake-like. The two amphibians on the back rocks are known as *Urocordylus*, and Burian suggests that they were insect-eaters.

I-Spy 25 for Microbrachis, *35 for* Branchiosaurus, *35 for* Dolichosoma, *35 for* Urocordylus

Cacops

Large amphibians, such as the labyrinthodonts, lived on land and in the water. Some were rather crocodile-like in appearance whereas others were heavily built and squat land dwellers. The labyrinthodonts had strong teeth and backbones, and a few kinds resembled reptiles. *Cacops* from the Permian (285-245 mya) was an example of a sturdy limbed labyrinthodont.

I-Spy for 35

Moschops

Reptiles first appeared in the Late Carboniferous, 315 million years ago. It was not until the Permian, however, that these animals became important in the various communities of animals. The ancestors of the dinosaurs, ichthyosaurs, and turtles had evolved by the end of the Permian. One group would also give rise to the mammals. The so-called mammal-like reptiles included *Moschops*. This heavily built plant-eater had a rather awkward-looking appearance. The skull was short, and the jaws had peg-like teeth. *Moschops* was 2.4 metres (8 ft) long.

I-Spy for **25**

Mesosaurus

Among the early reptiles from the beginning of the Permian was *Mesosaurus*. It was about 70 centimetres (28 in) in length and had a long, slim body. The head was extended into a long snout armed with many sharp, slightly curved teeth. *Mesosaurus* was a very efficient fish-eater. The limbs were modified for swimming and the feet may have been webbed; the tail was long and deep. Mesosaurs are the earliest-known sea-dwelling reptiles, and many skeletons have been collected from Permian rocks of southern Africa and South America.

I-Spy for **25**

Dimetrodon

Dimetrodon, a sail lizard, was a ferocious meat-eater whereas *Edaphosaurus* ate plants. It is thought that both animals used the large dorsal fin to control their body temperatures. In the early morning, the sail lizard would stand at right-angles to the sun so that the fin gathered heat to warm the animal's body. In the heat of the day, heat could be lost through the fin if the animal turned head on to the sun, allowing any breeze to cool the surface. Skeletons of *Dimetrodon* are among the most common exhibits in museum collections. Models and reconstructions are also popular in theme parks.

*I-Spy **15** for a skeleton,*
***5** for a model*

Lycaenops

By Late Permian times, the battle for survival among the various groups was approaching a climax. The mammal-like reptiles, such as *Lycaenops*, were very successful. They were rather more agile than many of their contemporaries, low slung, and strongly built. *Lycaenops* had sabre-like teeth at the front of its jaws. It was an efficient killer. There is evidence to suggest that these mammal-like reptiles were warm blooded and even covered with hair.
I-Spy for 25

Pareiasaurus

Among the prey of the meat-eaters were rather primitive reptiles, such as *Pareiasaurus*. It grew to 2.4 metres (8 ft) in length and was heavily built. The limbs were spread out from the body, and the animal moved slowly across the ground. The head was broad but the teeth were small and saw edged. These were ideal for eating plants but they would have been useless for defence.
I-Spy for 15

Lystrosaurus

Perhaps the best known of all the mammal-like reptiles is *Lystrosaurus*. It was distributed widely during the Early Triassic. It is known from South Africa, India, China, and the Antarctic. It provides evidence for a huge southern landmass 245 million years ago. *Lystrosaurus* was short and broad with strong legs and a short tail. The head was quite large with a short snout, large eyes, and a tusk-like tooth on either side of the upper jaw. *Lystrosaurus* made up 90 per cent of the backboned animals of the southern continent at this time. Among its enemies were the cynodonts or 'dog-tooth' reptiles. These were lightly built, agile hunters, including *Thrinaxodon* and *Cynognathus*.

I-Spy for **15**

37

Nothosaur

The nothosaurs were an important group of reptiles during the Triassic. They were sea goers, living along the coastlines of shallow seas. Fossils have been found in Germany, Switzerland, England, France, Holland, Poland, the Middle East, and Asia. The different kinds ranged in length from 20 centimetres (8 in) to 4 metres (13 ft). A typical nothosaur had a relatively long, narrow head, a long neck and body, and a fairly deep tail. The limbs were paddle-

like, indicating that these animals were good swimmers. The discovery in Switzerland of a tiny skeleton, just over 4 centimetres (2 in) long, may suggest that nothosaurs laid their eggs in nests on land. *I-Spy 15 for any nothosaur, 25 for another 'fish lizard'* Mixosaurus

Longisquama

Among the spectacular reptiles of the Late Triassic is *Longisquama*. Its name means 'long scale' clearly referring to the elongated scales that were present along the back edges of th arms, the legs, and over th animal's back. *Longisquama* was a glider. When it walked on land, it held the double rows of huge scales above the back vertically. It would launch itself into the air, with the back scales held out horizontally, to function as gliding wings. Remains of *Longisquama* have been found in central Asia. There are other Triassic gliders known from North America.

I-Spy for **35**

Hyperodapedon

By the end of the Triassic Period, the dinosaurs had effectively eliminated the opposition including most mammal-like reptiles and the more primitive reptilian stocks. In some areas of the world, however, the lizards, snakes, and their relatives, the rhynchosaurs, flourished. Remains of important communities of these animals have been discovered in Brazil, Germany, and from Scotland where *Hyperodapedon* has been found. It was a plant-eater that lived on horsetails and ferns.

I-Spy **15** *for any rhynchosaur*   **25** *for* Hyperodapedon

Muraenosaurus

The Cretaceous seas teemed with life. Many of the groups that had first appeared during the Jurassic survived but some, like the plesiosaurs and ichthyosaurs, were fewer in numbers and less varied. Among the plesiosaurs, giants such as *Muraenosaurus* thrived, with adult individuals reaching 14 metres (46 ft) in length. *Muraenosaurus* was an elasmosaur, a plesiosaur with a very long neck. It had over 70 individual bones in its neck alone. This made the neck very flexible and gave the animal an advantage when feeding. Mostly, it fed on fish but occasionally it could snatch a low-flying pterosaur from the sky just above the surface of the waves.

I-Spy 5 for any plesiosaur   *35 for* Muraenosaurus

Pteranodon

Pteranodon was a very large tailless pterosaur from the Upper Cretaceous. It had a long toothless beak and a crest. The crest probably kept the head upright as this large creature dived down over the sea in search of food. It is likely that *Pteranodon* soared on rising air currents. It had an 8-metre (26-ft) wingspan. Probably, *Pteranodon* lived close to the edges of high cliffs, and to fly it would launch itself seawards and then glide upwards.
I-Spy for 15

More Pterosaurs

Many of the Jurassic pterosaurs were small and agile fliers. *Rhamphorhynchus* had a small head and a long tail whereas *Dimorphodon* was a grotesque, big-headed animal. The tailless *Pterodactylus* probably hung from branches in a bat-like way.

I-Spy 25 for Rhamphorhynchus,
15 for Dimorphodon,
25 for Pterodactylus

Mosasaurus and *Tylosaurus*

Among the great battles that took place in the seas of the Upper Cretaceous was between a huge plesiosaur and the ferocious 'Meuse lizard' *Mosasaurus*. The mosasaurs were distant cousins of snakes and lizards. They were huge creatures compared with their living relatives, with *Mosasaurus* and the American form, *Tylosaurus*, reaching 8 metres (26 ft) in length. The head was large and armed with dozens of vicious teeth. *Mosasaurus* powered through the water by thrashing its long flattened tail. The small flippers were used for steering the animal as it pursued its prey. For a short time, these animals dominated the Cretaceous seas. *Mosasaurus* was well adapted for killing; the strangely built skull and short neck enabled it to grapple with its prey and rip the unfortunate victim to pieces. Apart from other backboned animals, ammonites, octopuses, and squids form the mainstay of a mosasaur's diet.

I-Spy 15 for Mosasaurus

I-Spy 35 for Tylosaurus

Ichthyosaur

During the Cretaceous, other marine reptiles, such as the ichthyosaurs (fish lizards) and the short-necked pliosaurs, were present in limited numbers. The ichthyosaurs were particularly abundant during the Lower Jurassic, and hundreds of skeletons have been found in Liassic rocks of England and Germany. Among the pliosaurs, forms such as *Kronosaurus* persisted into the Lower Cretaceous times in Australia.

The model of an ichthyosaur at Crystal Palace is quite accurate but it is unlikely that the fish lizards ever came too close inshore. It is thought that they gave birth to live young rather than laying eggs.

I-Spy for **5**

Geosaurus

Of all the living reptiles, snakes, lizards, turtles, and crocodiles are the ones we know best. The first crocodiles appeared during the Triassic (245-208 mya). They have the same ancestors as the dinosaurs and pterosaurs. During the Jurassic (208-144 mya), various forms invaded the seas. Some were successful. *Geosaurus*, for example, had paddle-like limbs and a tail like that of a fish. It was a powerful swimmer, and had a long snout armed with many sharp teeth.

I-Spy for 25

Turtles and Tortoises

The turtles and tortoises can also be traced as far back as the Triassic. At first, they probably lived in lakes or ponds but, eventually, they adapted to various environments. Sea turtles first evolved during the Late Jurassic and Early Cretaceous. By Late Cretaceous times, the ancestors of today's green turtles and leathery turtles had appeared. The skull shown is that of a leathery turtle from Eocene (55-38 mya) rocks of North Africa.

I-Spy 5 for a turtle or tortoise

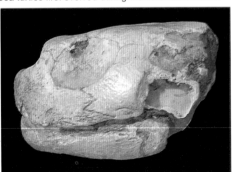

Diatryma

At the end of the Cretaceous, the dinosaurs vanished from the face of the Earth. Their extinction allowed other animals to flourish and occupy vacant niches. Among these was *Diatryma*, a huge flightless bird. We know that birds evolved from a dinosaurian ancestor. *Diatryma* was almost as fearless and ferocious as *Tyrannosaurus rex*. It is known as the 'terror crane' and, at 2 metres (over 6 ft) tall, it was a formidable foe. It had a large, parrot-like beak and huge clawed feet. *Diatryma* was the scourge of the North American mammals of the Tertiary (65-2 mya).

I-Spy for 15

Sabre-tooth Cats

Mammals have dominated our planet for the last 65 million years. Different kinds have evolved on land and in the sea so that, in some ways, their history is every bit as exciting as that of the dinosaurs. Sabre-tooth tigers and mammoths are well-known fossil mammals. They are relatively recent arrivals. The history of warm-blooded creatures that gave birth to live young stretches back to Triassic times (about 210 million years ago). The first meat-eaters (carnivores)

appeared about 60 mya. The big sabre-tooth cats, such as *Homotherium* and *Smilodon*, were the scourge of Late Pliocene to Early Pleistocene (5-2 mya) plant-eaters. They probably fed on animals like the giant tree sloth or perhaps on the ancestors of modern mammals.

I-Spy 25 for Homotherium ☐ *or 15 for* Smilodon ☐

Woolly Mammoth

The woolly mammoth was a giant. It stood over 3 metres (10 ft) tall and had huge curved tusks. The body was covered with thick brown hair and a woolly underfur. Mammoth graveyards have been discovered in the arctic tundra of Siberia.

I-Spy for 5 ☐